Mommy's Little Helper Christmas Crafts

Cynthia MacGregor

 **Meadowbrook Press**

**Distributed by Simon & Schuster
New York**

Library of Congress Cataloging-in-Publication Data
MacGregor, Cynthia.
      Mommy's little helper Christmas crafts / Cynthia MacGregor; illustrated by Glenn
Quist.
            p.   cm.
      ISBN 0-88166-345-X (Meadowbrook)—ISBN 0-689-83071-8 (Simon & Schuster)
      1. Christmas decorations.   I. Title.
TT900.C4M23   1999
745.594'12—dc21   99-41364
                                                        CIP

Editor: Christine Zuchora-Walske
Production Manager: Joe Gagne
Desktop Publishing: Danielle White
Illustrations: Glenn Quist

Published by Meadowbrook Press, 5451 Smetana Drive, Minnetonka, Minnesota
55343

www.meadowbrookpress.com

BOOK TRADE DISTRIBUTION by Simon & Schuster, a division of Simon and Schuster,
Inc., 1230 Avenue of the Americas, New York, NY 10020

03 02 01 00 99   10 9 8 7 6 5 4 3 2 1

Printed in the United States of America

DEDICATION

For Laurel and the kids . . . always.

ACKNOWLEDGMENTS

As always, my thanks to Vic Bobb,
a good writer and a good friend, for his help.

CONTENTS

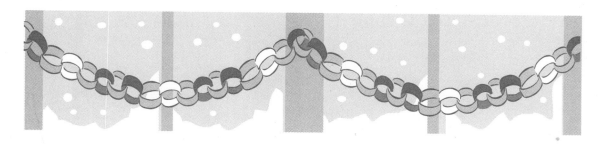

INTRODUCTION

Christmas. It's a time of excitement and warm, cozy pleasures: friends and family visiting . . . cookies and pies baking in the oven . . . your kids' eyes sparkling as they anticipate the pile of presents under your tree on Christmas morning. Shopping is worth the hassle when you imagine the delight you'll see as the wrappings come off the packages. The glow in your heart will be as bright as all the lights on your tree put together.

And now, here's another pleasure you can relish during the holiday season: creating Christmas crafts with your young child. The crafts in this book will deck your halls with a charming, homespun look . . . and best of all, your child will be able to proclaim proudly, "Mommy and I made these together. I really, really helped!"

You don't have to be an expert crafter—nor do you need any specialized materials—to do the projects in *Mommy's Little Helper Christmas Crafts.* Every craft is accompanied by helpful illustrations and divided into simple steps, each of which is marked clearly for mommy 👩 or child 🙂 . The only materials you'll need are ordinary objects and basic crafting supplies like scissors, tape, construction paper, and a glue gun.

I'm confident that you'll find the crafts in this book easy and rewarding. You and your child will have a ball making them together. Your whole family will enjoy the cozy, festive look they add to your home during the holidays. Best of all, your child will be proud to share in the credit for their creation.

Merry Christmas!

Cynthia

SHOW IT OFF!

CANDY CANE CONTAINER

This container serves a double purpose: It's a lovely decoration for your shelf, mantel, or coffee table and it also makes a great holder for pencils, marbles, and other small items. If you stick a sprig or two of evergreen in this container, it also makes a great holiday vase.

Time: 15 minutes

Materials:
- Large, clean, empty can
- Large bowl of water
- Towel
- Glue
- Box of candy canes whose length equals or exceeds the depth of the can
- Ribbon, approximately 12 inches long
- Green crepe paper (optional)
- Scissors (optional)

What to Do:

 1. Check a large, empty can for sharp edges; smooth any that you find.

2. Soak the can in water until the label comes off.

3. Thoroughly dry the can with a towel.

4. Apply glue to the outside of the can.

5. Attach candy canes to the glue, hiding all the metal. (The candy hooks should stick out away from the can.)

6. Tie a ribbon around the can at the midpoint of the canes. If you like, put a few dabs of glue on the ribbon so it will stick to the canes.

7. Make a pretty bow from the ends of the ribbon.

Tip: Choose a green ribbon unless you've used green crepe paper (see Creative Option below), in which case your best choice is a gold or silver ribbon.

Creative Option: Cut a piece of green crepe paper to fit around the can, and glue it in place after Step 4. Then glue 4 to 6 candy canes to the crepe paper at regular intervals. Make sure the candy canes also adhere to the top and bottom edges of the can for a better grip. (If the canes stick only to the crepe paper, they may tear the paper and fall off.)

CHRISTMAS COLLAGE

This project recycles last year's Christmas cards into this year's decoration. The finished product is suitable for framing and hanging on a wall, in a window, or on the inside of a door.

Time: about 45 minutes (varies depending on the complexity of your collage)

Materials:
- Large piece of cardboard, at least 8 inches by 10 inches (the larger the better)
- Green paint and paintbrush
- Old Christmas cards
- Scissors
- Glue
- Brown construction paper (optional)

What to Do:

 1. Paint cardboard with green paint.

 2. While the paint dries, cut out pictures from old Christmas cards—a Santa, a reindeer (or a whole team of them), a sleigh, a snow-covered house, and so on.

3. Arrange the pictures onto the cardboard so they overlap each other. Any parts of the cardboard not covered will look like a Christmasy green background.

Creative Option: Make a frame from brown construction paper. Cut 4 strips of paper of equal width that match the sides of the cardboard in length. Glue the strips to the edges of the collage.

Tip: If you are going to frame your collage, leave a border when you arrange your pictures.

4. Glue the pictures in place.

CHRISTMAS PARTY CLOTH

This festive cloth is more than just a Christmas decoration. It is also a fun activity for two or more people, so it makes a great party game. If creating this cloth at a party, plan to have your child and his guests work on the cloth early on. Then spread the cloth out on the table when it's time for the goodies to be served!

Hint: You can also adapt this craft activity for birthday parties.

Time: Varies, depending on the complexity of the design

Materials:
- Newspapers
- White or pastel sheet (any size)
- Masking tape
- Permanent color markers

What to Do:

 1. Spread newspapers out on the floor, and put the sheet down on top of them. Be sure the whole area under the sheet is covered with newspapers.

 2. Tape the corners of the sheet to the floor.

 3. Draw Christmasy pictures on the sheet.

4. Write Christmas greetings like "Happy Holidays!" "Ho, Ho, Ho!" and "Santa's coming!" on the sheet.

 5. Sign your name on the sheet.

Tips: If your child isn't old enough to sign his name, help him form his initials.

Since the markers are permanent, you can throw this cloth in the wash to remove stains without losing the design. You'll be able to use it again and again!

FAMILY PICTURE FRAME

Whether you use this frame as a home decoration or give it as a holiday gift, you'll have a ball making it. Take a favorite family photo, spiff it up with a homemade frame, and you've got a decoration that everyone will love!

Time: 20 minutes

Materials:
- Piece of sturdy cardboard at least 2 inches wider and 2 inches taller than the picture you've chosen
- Scissors
- Ruler
- Glue
- Pretty wrapping paper
- Family photo, preferably 4 inches by 5 inches
- Pencil
- Utility knife

What to Do:

 1. Trim a piece of sturdy cardboard so it exceeds the size of the picture you've chosen by 1 inch on all sides.

 2. Glue wrapping paper to 1 side of the cardboard. Trim to fit.

 3. Center a family picture on the plain side of the cardboard, and trace around it. Now draw another rectangle within the first rectangle. Make the second rectangle ¼ inch smaller on all sides.

4. With a utility knife, carefully cut out the smaller rectangle.

5. **Apply glue to the area between the cut rectangle and the larger rectangle.**

6. Place the photo within the large rectangle, with the picture facing away from you. Press in place.

7. Cut another piece of sturdy cardboard (corrugated is best) approximately 4 inches by 4 inches, and fold it in half. Unfold to make a tent shape.

8. **Holding the folded edge upward, glue one side of the cardboard tent to the bottom of the frame's back. Prop it up. It's finished!**

GLITTERY PINE CONES

Pine cones say winter, no question about it. And winter says . . . Christmas! No wonder pine cones are popular Christmas decorations. Spruce up some ordinary pine cones to greet the holiday cheerily. You'll be seeing sparkles all over your house if you follow these instructions. Santa will feel right at home when he arrives!

Time: 30 minutes

Materials:
- Newspaper
- 6 pine cones
- Gold and silver spray paint
- Glue
- Gold and silver glitter

What to Do:

 1. Spread newspaper over your work surface.

2. Spray-paint 2 pine cones with silver paint and 2 with gold paint. Leave the other 2 unpainted.

3. When the paint is dry, apply glue in a pattern all over the silver cones, then sprinkle the cones with gold glitter. Don't glob the glitter in clumps.

4. Apply silver glitter in the same manner to the gold cones.

 6. When the glue is dry, shake each cone sharply a couple of times over the newspaper to dislodge any loose glitter. Your cones are now ready to display.

5. Apply glue to the unpainted cones. Pick up the mixed gold and silver glitter that has fallen to the newspaper covering your work surface and sprinkle it on the cones. If that isn't enough glitter, add more of both colors.

MINIATURE CHRISTMAS TREES

Here's an easy decoration to make, and one that you will enjoy both creating and looking at afterward.

Time: 10 or 15 minutes, depending on how you choose to decorate your "tree"

Materials:
- Jar lid slightly bigger than the base of the pine cone
- Aluminum foil
- Glue
- Large pine cone
- Paint, tinsel, glitter, and/or sequins

What to Do:

 1. Cover a clean jar lid with aluminum foil.

 2. Put some glue on the top of the foil-covered lid. Then place the base of the pine cone onto the glue. Let dry.

 3. Decorate the cone: paint it, drape it with tinsel, or glue glitter or sequins on it. Be creative.

RICE KRISPIE TREES

If your child loves Rice Krispie treats, the main feature of this decoration, you may want to make a double batch—one to work with and one to eat while you're working!

Time: 10 minutes, after you've made the Rice Krispie treats

Materials:
- A batch of Rice Krispie treats
- 1 paper plate per tree
- Christmas M&Ms (in red and green)
- Hershey's Christmas Kisses (in silver or gold foil)

What to Do:

 1. Make a batch of Rice Krispie treats according to the instructions on the Rice Krispies box.

 2. **Form the Rice Krispie treats into Christmas tree shapes on paper plates.**

3. **Decorate each tree with red and green M&Ms. Use a foil-wrapped Hershey's Kiss for a star.**

ROCKIN' SANTA

Hey, guess what? Santa really rocks! At least this Santa does; he's made from a rock. This project's easy and fun, and the result is an early visit from the jolly man himself. Ho, ho, ho—Santa's already at your house!

Time: 30 minutes

Materials:
- 1 smooth, flat rock (round or oval in shape)
- Paint and paintbrush
- Cotton balls
- Glue
- Red felt
- Scissors

What to Do:

1. **Wash a rock and let it dry thoroughly.**

2. **Paint a Santa face—eyes, nose, and red cheeks (no mouth, as the mustache and beard will cover it)—onto the rock.**

3. **Use cotton balls to make a mustache and beard, as well as tufts of white hair. Glue in place.**

4. Cut out a stocking cap (cone shape) from red felt. This hat is one flat piece to be glued to the surface of the rock.

5. Glue the cap in place on Santa's head.

6. Attach a small cotton ball to the tip of the cap.

7. Smooth out the cap and set the Santa aside to dry.

SANTA'S SLEIGH

Santa's going for a ride . . . right through your house. Create his sleigh as a decoration for your mantel or a centerpiece to grace your table.

Time: 15 minutes

Materials:
- Newspapers
- Rectangular box about 6 to 10 inches long
- Scissors
- Red spray paint
- Approximately 7 small square or oblong pieces of Styrofoam or tiny boxes
- Gift wrap
- Transparent tape

What to Do:

1. Spread newspapers over your work surface.

2. Cut the 2 long sides of the box to look like the sides of a sleigh. The exact proportions will depend on the size of the box.

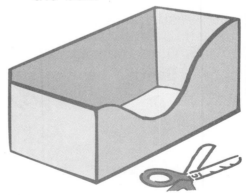

3. Spray-paint the box with red paint. Let dry.

 4. Cover Styrofoam pieces or small boxes with gift wrap.

5. Tape the gift wrap in place.

 6. Place the tiny gifts in the sleigh and use as a centerpiece or other decoration.

STYROFOAM SNOWMAN

Bring a little winter wonder indoors with this snowman ornament. He'll happily perch on your coffee table, dining room table, bookcase, or knickknack shelf. Best of all, he won't melt!

Time: 30 minutes

Materials:
- 5 toothpicks
- 2 Styrofoam balls (from craft shop)
- Approximately 17 cloves
- Small piece of cardboard or black construction paper
- Scissors
- 1 cork
- Glue
- Black marker

What to Do:

 1. Insert 2 toothpicks close together into 1 Styrofoam ball, then press the other Styrofoam ball onto the toothpicks, stacking the balls to resemble the head and body of a snowman.

 2. **Use 2 cloves for the snowman's eyes, 1 clove for the nose, and a curved line of 7 cloves for a smiling mouth. Place 3 cloves in a straight line on the body for buttons.**

3. Place 4 cloves in a square on the bottom of the snowman to form a base for balance.

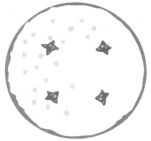

 6. Push a toothpick into the bottom of the hat. Stick the other end of the toothpick into the snowman's head to attach the hat.

 7. Push a toothpick into each side of the snowman's body to make arms. Your snowman is now finished.

4. Cut and glue a circle of cardboard or black construction paper to a cork to create a hat.

 5. If you use cardboard, color it black with a marker. Then color the cork black, too.

TANNENBAUM TOPPER

This decoration will really brighten up your Christmas dinner. If you'll be serving a covered dish, you can slip this Christmas tree over the knob of the lid. Because it uses glitter, keep it away from uncovered food.

Time: 10 minutes

Materials:
- Green construction paper
- Scissors
- Glue
- Brightly colored construction paper
- Hole punch
- Glitter pen or glue and glitter

What to Do:

1. Lay a piece of green construction paper in front of you with a short side nearest to you. Fold the paper in half so the open side faces you.

2. Cut upward from each bottom corner to form a triangle whose point is in the middle of the folded edge. Glue the 2 cut sides together to form a cone shape from the triangle. Let dry.

3. Use the hole punch to make many small circles of brightly colored construction paper. Glue the circles onto the green cone to look like ornaments on a Christmas tree.

4. Slip the tree over two fingers and lightly draw garlands on it with a glitter pen, or draw lines on it with glue and sprinkle glitter on the glue. Shake off any excess glitter.

5. Place the tannenbaum topper over the knob on the lid of a covered dish.

GIFTY TRIVET

You can recycle old metal bottle caps into a useful trivet that's as pretty as a Christmas present!

Time: 40 minutes

Materials:
- Square or rectangular piece of heavy cardboard
- Glue
- Metal bottle caps of a uniform height
- Poster paints and paintbrush

What to Do:

1. Glue the tops of the bottle caps onto 1 side of the cardboard. Place the caps close to each other and cover the entire side of the cardboard. Let dry.

2. Paint the entire trivet—all the bottle caps and cardboard—to look like a wrapped Christmas gift.

HANG IT UP!

BE-LEAF IT OR NOT, IT'S SANTA

Leaves form the basis of this unusual picture, with berries and seeds making up the balance. Be-leaf it or not, you can create a Santa from these natural objects!

Time: 20 minutes

Materials:

- 2 red poinsettia leaves and 1 round or oval brown or green leaf
- Glue
- Sheet of white construction paper
- Scissors
- Seeds, seed pods, twigs, berries, spices, or dried vegetables—whatever nature or your cupboards have to offer
- Cotton balls

What to Do:

1. Glue a red poinsettia leaf in the middle of the sheet of paper and glue a smaller green or brown leaf directly above it. These are Santa's body and head.

2. Cut a red poinsettia leaf in half across the middle.

3. Glue the half leaf just over the top of Santa's head, with the pointy end up and the flat end overlapping the head. This is Santa's hat.

4. Glue berries or seeds to the head for eyes and a nose. Make a mouth from a small twig, a line of seeds, or even a dried lima bean.

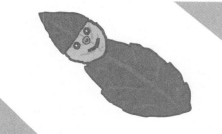

 6. Add arms and legs using long, thin leaves, twigs, seed pods, cinnamon sticks, or whatever seems suitable. Add seeds for buttons down the front of the body.

 **5.** Tear cotton balls into tufts and glue to Santa's face for a mustache and beard. Glue a cotton ball to the tip of the hat and a strip of cotton to the base of the hat.

CANDY CANE HEARTS

Though hearts are usually thought of as Valentine's Day decorations, Christmas is also a season of love. Have you heard of wearing your heart on your sleeve? Here's a heart that your tree, your front door, or your mantel can wear!

Time: 10 minutes

Materials:
- 2 large candy canes
- Glue
- 8-inch-long red or white ribbon
- White lace (optional)

What to Do:

1. Place 2 large candy canes on a flat work surface, hooks inward so that the tips join to form a heart shape. Apply glue to the tips of the candy canes and hold them together briefly. Let them dry.

2. Tie a red or white ribbon in a knot at the top of the heart, leaving 2 long ends. Tie the ends again, making a loop from which to hang the heart.

 3. Hang the heart on the tree, door handle, or anywhere you like.

Creative Option: Apply a thin layer of glue along the outside edge of the heart and attach white lace for a Victorian effect.

Instead of hanging the heart, tie the ribbon into a decorative bow and prop the heart up on a shelf, table, or any other surface.

CHRISTMAS MOBILE

This project is a great way to recycle your old Christmas cards! If you don't have any on hand, save this year's cards to make a mobile next year.

Time: 30 minutes to several hours

Materials:

- Old Christmas cards
- Scissors
- Cardboard
- Glue
- Red and green or gold and silver crayons or paint
- Nylon thread
- Dowel or hanger
- Red and green construction paper or Christmas wrap (optional)

What to Do:

 1. Look through old Christmas cards for large Christmas figures such as Santa, reindeer, Christmas trees, doves, elves, and so on.

 2. Cut out the Christmas figures.

 3. Glue the cutouts to cardboard. Let dry.

 4. Cut out each cardboard-backed figure.

 5. Decorate the cardboard side of each figure with green and red or gold and silver crayons or paint.

6. Make a small hole at the top of each figure. Tie different lengths of thread to the figures.

7. **Lay the figures out in any order you like.**

8. Tie all the figures to the rod or hanger.

Creative Option: Instead of decorating the backs of the figures with paint or crayon, trace around them on construction paper. Cut out the traced shapes and glue them to the backs of the figures.

Tips: If you don't have old Christmas cards, never fear. Glue red and green construction paper or Christmas wrap (preferably used) onto both sides of a sheet of cardboard. Then draw and cut out various seasonal shapes, such as candles, stars, Christmas trees, or sleighs.

To balance a mobile made with a dowel, tie a length of thread to both ends.

CHRISTMAS MOSAIC

This easy project will result in a cheery, festive decoration to brighten your holidays.

Time: 15 to 20 minutes

Materials:
- 1 sheet of white construction paper
- Pencil
- Several sheets of colored construction paper
- Glue
- Double-sided tape

What to Do:

 1. On a sheet of white construction paper, draw an outline of a simple holiday picture. This might be a Christmas tree, a star, or a snowman, for example.

MERRY CHRISTMAS

 2. Below the picture, in outlined block letters, write "MERRY CHRISTMAS" or any other appropriate holiday sentiment.

 3. Tear colored construction paper into bits.

4. Carefully apply glue to a small area of the picture or 1 letter. Cover the glue with bits of torn paper. Continue in this way until the whole picture and all the letters are covered with colorful paper bits. Let dry.

**5.** Hang the mosaic on a wall, door, or window using double-sided tape.

MERRY CHRISTMAS

ELF WALL HANGING

Teamwork is needed for this project. By working together, you and your child can create a wall hanging so eye-catching that your child may want to leave it hanging in his room all year round. (After all, not all elves are Christmas elves!)

Time: 1 hour

Materials:
- 2-by-3-foot piece of burlap
- Brightly colored rickrack
- Glue
- Needle and thread
- Buttons
- Felt, different colors
- Scraps of fake fur

What to Do:

 1. Divide the burlap into sections by gluing strips of rickrack across it. A good size for each section is 1 foot by 1 foot, which would give you 6 squares.

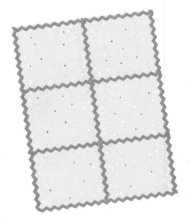

 2. Sew 2 buttons (for the elves' eyes) in each section. Cut out different-shaped noses, mouths, hats, and rosy cheeks from felt. Cut fake fur into strips or tufts for hair.

 3. Glue the noses, mouths, hats, rosy cheeks, and hair in place.

4. Hang the elves in the family room or child's room.

GLITTERY SNOWFLAKES

Why should snowflakes glitter only outside and melt when you bring them indoors? These snowflakes won't turn into a puddle, so you can enjoy them day after day.

Time: 20 to 30 minutes, depending on the number of snowflakes

Materials:
- 1 sheet of blue construction paper
- Pencil
- Glue
- Silver glitter

What to Do:

1. Draw several snowflakes with pencil on a sheet of blue construction paper.

2. Spread glue over the pencil lines of 1 snowflake.

3. Sprinkle glitter onto the glue.

4. Shake the paper gently from side to side to completely coat the glue with glitter.

5. Gently shake off any excess glitter.

6. Repeat steps 2–5 for the remaining snowflakes.

MOCK STAINED-GLASS ORNAMENT

This mock stained-glass ornament will sparkle hanging next to the twinkle lights on your Christmas tree.

Time: 15 minutes to 1 hour, depending on complexity of design

Materials:
- Small piece of lightweight cardboard
- Scissors
- Aluminum foil
- Tape
- Colored and black permanent markers
- Plastic wrap
- Double-faced tape or glue
- Large, heavy needle and thread

What to Do:

 1. Cut 2 identical cardboard circles and 2 pieces of foil a couple of inches larger than the circles.

 2. **Crumple the foil so it's wrinkly, then uncrumple it.**

 3. **Cover each cardboard circle with wrinkled foil. Fold the foil over the edges and tape it down on the back of each circle.**

4. Tape 2 pieces of plastic wrap to your work surface so that they are taut. Each plastic wrap piece should be about the same size as the foil pieces.

 5. **Use a black marker to draw a design on each piece of plastic wrap. Color the designs with colorful markers.**

 6. Tape the plastic wrap over the circles in the same way that the foil was taped. Then join the 2 circles back-to-back with double-faced tape or glue.

 7. With a large, heavy needle, attach a loop of thread to the top of the ornament.

 8. **Hang the ornament on your twinkly Christmas tree!**

POMANDER BALLS

After this pomander performs its holiday duty, you can retire it to your linen closet to let it scent your sheets and towels. You'll need to create your pomander ball about a month before you actually want to use it.

Time: 20 to 30 minutes, plus 1 month to dry

Materials:
- Large orange
- 2 ounces of whole cloves
- 1-foot piece and 6-inch piece of festive ribbon
- Darning needle and thimble (optional)

What to Do:

1. Starting at the top of the orange, insert 4 cloves in a tight circle (it will really look more like a square), touching each other.

2. **Stud the entire orange with cloves, keeping the cloves tightly spaced. Start just below the first 4 cloves and work your way down the orange in ever-widening circles.**

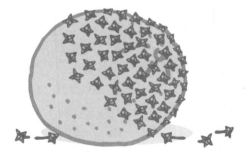

3. Store the pomander ball in a warm, dry place— a closet or cupboard will do fine—for about a month. Don't worry

about spoilage; the cloves will preserve the orange while it dries and shrinks.

 4. **Place the orange in the middle of the 1-foot piece of ribbon.**

 5. Tie the ends of the ribbon in a bow at the top of the orange.

 6. **Run the 6-inch piece of ribbon under the bow.**

 7. Tie the extra ribbon into a loop.

 8. **Hang the pomander ball from your Christmas tree, a plant hook, or a cabinet knob.**

Tips: You can make insertion of the cloves a little easier if you first pierce a hole in the orange with a thick darning needle. You'll probably want to use a thimble with the darning needle.

Hold the studded orange carefully to avoid breaking off the cloves. Save leftover cloves to replace any that break.

POPCORN CHRISTMAS TREE

Create a picture of a Christmas tree using popcorn for the ornaments! This is one project you'll be tempted to eat, so make a double batch of popcorn— half for snacking and half for decorating.

Time: 20 minutes

Materials:
- Newspaper
- Red and green food coloring
- 2 small bowls
- Popped popcorn
- Brown construction paper
- Scissors
- White construction or typing paper
- Glue
- Paint and paintbrush or crayons

What to Do:

1. Spread newspapers over your work surface.

2. In 1 bowl, place red food coloring. In another, put green food coloring.

3. Dip half of the popcorn in the red coloring and the other half in the green. Dunk it completely to coat it well. Set the popcorn aside on the newspaper to dry.

4. Cut a frame out of brown construction paper and glue it to the sheet of white paper.

5. Within the frame, draw or paint a Christmas tree.

6. When the popcorn is dry, glue it to the tree to resemble ornaments and branches.

7. Hang your picture with pride!

QUILTED TREE ORNAMENTS

You will have tree-mendous fun creating these orna-ments, and they'll add a glam-orous touch to your tree. Even a novice can make this spiffy craft. You and your child will be able to say proudly, "We made those ourselves!"

Time: 20 minutes per ornament

Materials:
- Scraps of colorful material (cotton or cotton-polyester blend)
- Styrofoam balls
- Nail file with sharp point
- ⅜-inch-wide ribbon or pipe cleaners

What to Do:

 1. Cut fabric scraps into circles or ovals a few inches in diameter.

2. Lay 1 fabric piece on a Styrofoam ball.

3. Place the sharp tip of a nail file about ¼ inch from the edge of the fab-ric and poke the cloth into the Styrofoam, securing it in place. Work around the entire edge of the fabric in this manner, securing it to the ball.

 4. Select a contrasting piece of cloth and lay it on the ball so that part of its edge overlaps the first piece.

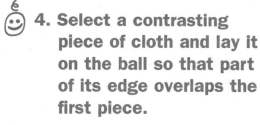 5. Poke the edges of the second piece into the Styrofoam with the nail file. Use the existing groove where the fabric pieces overlap.

 6. Continue adding pieces of fabric until the entire ball is covered.

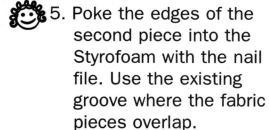 7. Hang the ball in one of the following ways: Push 1 end of a pipe cleaner into the top of the ball, then form a hook from the other end. Or loop a piece of ribbon and push the 2 ends into the top of the ball with a nail file.

SNOWY SAM

Snowy Sam is a big, jolly snowman who will greet your holiday visitors if you hang him on your front door. If your front door isn't protected from the elements, hang Sam on the inside of your front door or on an inside wall. He's a suitable decoration for the whole winter.

Time: 40 minutes

Materials:
- Pencil
- Posterboard
- Scissors
- Black permanent marker
- Cotton balls
- Glue
- Double-faced poster tape

What to Do:

 1. Use a pencil to draw a snowman on posterboard. Draw a top hat, a pipe, 2 eyes, 2 arms, and a nose.

 2. Cut out the snowman.

3. Use a permanent black marker to color in the pipe, eyes, nose, arms, and hat.

4. Glue cotton balls all over the snowman, except the black areas.

5. Proudly hang Sam on your door with double-faced poster tape.

STARRING SANTA

Ready for some holiday magic? Presto, change-o! Create a Santa out of a star.

Time: 30 minutes

Materials:
- Red, tan, black, and white construction paper
- Scissors
- Glue
- Cotton balls
- Crayons
- Needle and thread

What to Do:

 1. Cut a large 5-pointed star out of red paper.

 2. Draw a circle on tan paper. The circle should be big enough to cover the center of the star.

 3. Cut out the circle and place it in the center of the star.

 4. Glue the circle in place. The circle will be Santa's face. The top point will be Santa's cap, and the 4 other points will be his arms and legs.

5. Glue cotton all around the circle for Santa's beard and hatband. Glue cotton on the end of each point for Santa's cuffs and the pompom on his hat.

 6. Draw Santa's shoes on black paper and mittens on white paper.

7. Cut out the shoes and mittens and glue them in place on the appropriate points.

 8. Lay Santa flat and allow the glue to dry. When dry, use crayons to draw eyes, a nose, and a mouth on Santa's face.

 9. Use needle and thread to attach a loop to Santa's hat.

10. **Hang Santa from your Christmas tree, door, or curtain rod.**

STOCKING SANTA

Got a stocking whose mate is missing? Don't throw it out; turn it into a Santa and hang it on your front door or in your window.

Time: 20 to 30 minutes

Materials:
- Wire hanger
- Light-colored knee-high nylon stocking
- Pencil
- Red and blue construction paper
- Glue
- Cotton

What to Do:

 1. Bend a wire hanger into a circle. Leave the hook intact.

2. **Stretch an old stocking over the circle.**

3. Tie a knot in the open end of the stocking, leaving the hook sticking out.

4. **Draw a big, floppy hat on red paper. Draw 2 eyes on blue paper.**

5. Cut out the hat and eyes.

 6. **Glue the hat and eyes in place.**

 7. **Glue cotton balls to Santa's face for eyebrows, mustache, and beard. Glue a cotton pompom to the end of Santa's hat.**

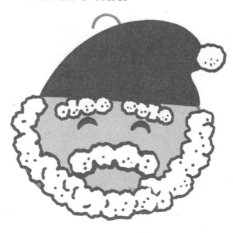

 8. Cut rosy cheeks and a mouth from red paper and glue them in place.

 9. **Hang Santa from his hook on your front door or in a window.**

TRADITIONAL POPCORN GARLANDS

Strings of popcorn are an old-fashioned tree or mantel decoration. Bring the tradition back to life with these festive garlands.

Time: 10 minutes per strand

Materials:
- Newspaper
- Darning needle
- Strong red and/or green thread
- Thimble
- Popcorn, popped
- Cranberries

What to Do:

1. Cover your work surface with newspaper.

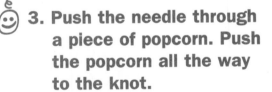

2. Thread a darning needle with a long strand of thread. Tie a double knot at the end.

3. Push the needle through a piece of popcorn. Push the popcorn all the way to the knot.

 4. Push the needle through a cranberry. Push the cranberry all the way to the piece of popcorn. Continue threading popcorn and cranberries alternately until the thread is filled. Leave enough thread at the end to tie a knot.

 5. Tie a knot at the end of the garland.

 6. Use popcorn garlands to trim your tree, to drape over doorways and across windows, and to decorate your mantel.

7. Eat any leftover popcorn!

NUTTY WREATH

Just for a change, here's a Christmas wreath that has no evergreen, holly, or red ribbon. Enjoy making it, then bask in the compliments.

Time: 20 to 30 minutes

Materials:
- Newspapers
- Can of gold spray paint
- 2 cups of assorted nuts still in their shells
- Small bunch of dried flowers
- 12-inch can or wicker wreath
- Glue

What to Do:

 1. Spread newspapers over your work surface.

2. Spray nuts and dried flowers thoroughly with gold paint. Set them aside to dry.

 3. Arrange gold nuts and flowers on a cane or wicker wreath.

 4. Glue items in place. Hang your wreath on a door or wall.

WINDOW DRESSINGS

CARDBOARD CANDLE

This Christmas candle will glow brightly yet safely in your window throughout the holiday season.

Time: 10 minutes

Materials:
- Yellow construction paper
- Pencil
- Scissors
- Glue
- Cardboard toilet-paper tube
- Red or green crepe paper
- Double-faced tape

What to Do:

 1. On the yellow paper, draw a flame about 2 inches wide and 3 inches tall. Draw a tab about 2 inches long and 1 inch wide below the flame.

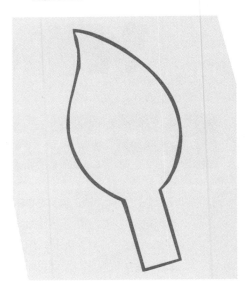

2. Cut out the flame. Erase any stray pencil marks on it. Cut a slit up the middle of the tab. Do not cut into the flame.

3. Pull 1 tab toward you and push 1 tab away from you. Hold the flame over the cardboard tube. Glue 1 tab to the inside front of the tube and the other tab to the inside back of the tube.

4. Cut a piece of crepe paper at least 8 inches square. Carefully cut a slit about 2 inches long in the center of the crepe paper.

 5. Apply glue to the outside of the tube. Poke the flame through the slit in the crepe paper, and pull the crepe paper down to cover the tube. Tuck the edges of the paper into the bottom of the tube.

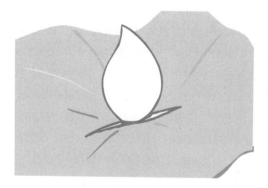

 6. Using double-faced tape, stick the candle to a windowpane or windowsill and let it shine for all to see!

MOCK STAINED-GLASS WINDOW

Stained glass windows are colorful, beautiful, and festive. Because they evoke the idea of churches, they act as a reminder that Christmas isn't just about Santa, snowmen, and presents. Be sure to hang this in a window that gets plenty of sunlight.

Time: Less than 30 minutes

Materials:
- 1 piece of black construction paper
- Pencil
- Scissors
- Glue
- 1 piece of onionskin paper
- Colored markers

What to Do:

1. With a pencil, draw several irregular shapes on the black paper. Make sure the shapes are at least a pinkie's width apart from each other and the edges of the paper.

2. Cut out the shapes, making sure not to not cut the paper between the shapes.

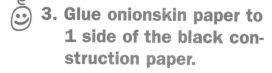 **3.** Glue onionskin paper to 1 side of the black construction paper.

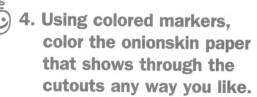 **4.** Using colored markers, color the onionskin paper that shows through the cutouts any way you like.

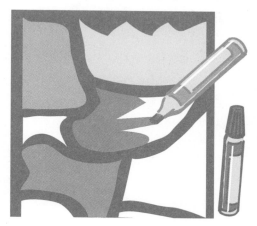

PAPER SNOWFLAKES

It's snowing indoors! But don't worry, these snow-flakes won't melt and leave puddles in your house. They're made of paper, and you can stick them to your windows to give winter joy to passersby.

Time: 5 minutes or less per snowflake

Materials:
- White typing paper
- Scissors

What to Do:

 1. Place a piece of typing paper in front of you. Fold so that 1 of the short edges lines up with an adjacent edge. Cut off the extra strip of paper, leaving a triangle.

 2. Fold the triangle so that 2 opposite corners meet. Now you'll have a smaller triangle. Fold again in the same way.

3. Cut wedges out of all 3 sides of the folded triangle. Be careful to leave some part of each side uncut. You'll get better results if you make many small cuts instead of a few large cuts.

4. Unfold the paper and hold it with 1 of the points facing up. It should resemble a snowflake.

5. Create additional snowflakes, then tape the snowflakes to your windows.

RECYCLED WINDOW BEADS

Hang these beads in your window at Christmastime. They'll be admired by all who see them! Save wrapping paper this year to use next year, do this project after Christmas, or make your beads from colorful pages of an old magazine.

Time: A few minutes per bead

Materials:
- Used Christmas wrap or an old magazine with colorful pictures
- Scissors
- Toothpick
- Glue
- Needle
- Dental floss

What to Do:

 1. Cut long, pennant-shaped triangles from old Christmas wrap or colorful magazine pages. The length of the fat end should be shorter than the length of a toothpick.

2. Lay a toothpick along the fat end of a triangle. Roll the triangle tightly around the toothpick with the colorful side out.

3. When the entire triangle is rolled up, place a small dab of glue on the point to seal the bead.

 5. Thread your beads with a needle and a length of dental floss longer than the width of the window in which the beads will be draped. Tie a knot at each end of the floss.

 6. Drape your string of beads across the window.

 4. Pull the toothpick out of the finished bead. Create more beads in the same way.

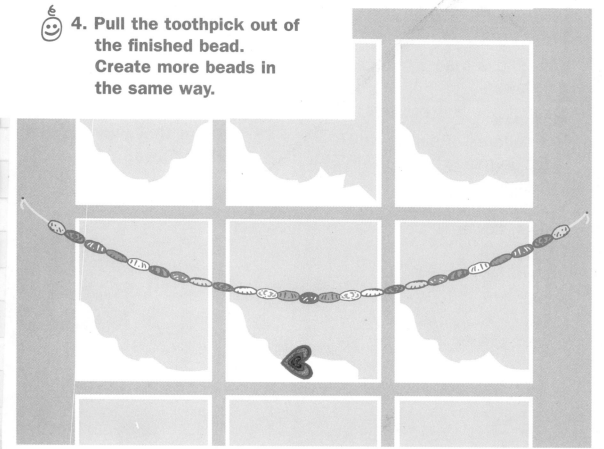

TISSUE FLOWER GARLAND

These flowers are made from tissue paper. Create them in red and green to remind you of poinsettias. The number of flowers you'll need will depend on the width of your window.

Time: Less than 5 minutes per flower

Materials:
- 4 squares of same-sized tissue paper for each flower
- 1 green pipe cleaner for each flower

What to Do:

 1. Place 4 squares of tissue paper together and fold them into tight accordion folds.

 2. **Wrap the end of a pipe cleaner around the middle of the folded sheets of tissue paper. Gently separate the sheets of tissue paper so that they puff out to form a flower.**

3. Make as many more flowers as you want.

5. Drape the garland across a window. Twist the ends around a curtain rod and let the garland droop well below the top of the window.

4. To form a garland of flowers, place the blossom of 1 flower about 2 inches below the blossom of another flower. Twist the stems together. Repeat until all your flowers are linked together.

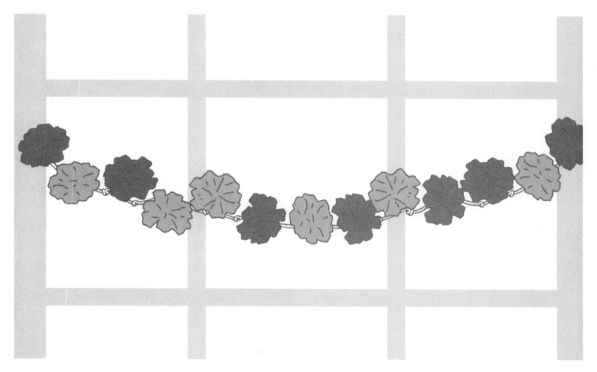

CHRISTMAS CHAINS

This project uses old Christmas wrap, so save your sturdy stuff this year. Next year you can turn it into paper chains to festoon your tree, windows, doorways, or walls.

Hint: On painted walls, use removable tape and press lightly to avoid disturbing any paint.

Time: A few minutes to a few hours, depending on length of chain

Materials:
- Scissors
- Sturdy Christmas wrap, preferably recycled, in as many patterns as possible
- Tape or glue

What to Do:

 1. Cut 1-by-6-inch strips of gift wrap.

 2. **Form a ring from 1 strip. Keep the patterned side out. Overlap 1 end over the other by ½ to 1 inch. Join the ends with glue or tape.**

 3. **Take a contrasting strip of paper, link it through the first ring, and join the ends. Continue adding links until the chain is as long as you want it.**

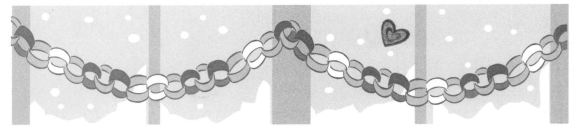

INVITATIONS

TREE-MENDOUS INVITATIONS

This unusual invitation opens at the top instead of the bottom!

Time: 10 to 20 minutes per invitation

Materials:
- 1 8½-by-11-inch sheet of scrap paper
- Pencil
- Scissors
- 1 8½-by-11-inch sheet of green construction paper for every 2 invitations
- Colored markers

What to Do:

1. Lay a sheet of scrap paper vertically in front of you. Fold it in half from top to bottom and again from side to side.

2. On the quarter-sheet now showing, draw a large Christmas tree, including a bit of trunk.

3. Cut out the tree. This will be your pattern. (You only need 1 of the 4 trees you've made.)

4. Lay a sheet of green paper vertically in front of you and fold it in half from bottom to top. The fold should face you.

 5. Lay the tree pattern on the green paper, as far to the left as possible. Place the bottom of the trunk flush with the fold. Trace the pattern, then place it on the right side of the paper and trace again.

 6. Cut each tree out. Be sure to cut through both layers of paper. Do not cut apart the fold.

 7. Decorate the outside of each tree. Use brown marker for the trunks and bright colors for ornaments.

 8. Write the party information (name, address, date, and time) on the inside of each invitation.

WRAP IT UP!

A GIFT WITH SPARKLE

Here's a sparkly alternative to plain old gift tags.

Time: 5 minutes

Materials:
- Glitter pen
  or
- Glue
- Glitter
- Newspaper

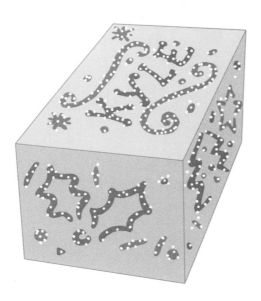

What to Do:

 1. Use a glitter pen to write the recipient's name on a gift box.

 2. Draw designs with a glitter pen on the rest of the box.

OR

 1. Spread newspapers over your work surface.

 2. Write the recipient's name in glue on the package.

 3. Sprinkle glitter over the glue.

 4. After the glue dries, shake off the excess glitter onto the newspaper. Tap the box against your work surface a few times to dislodge any loose glitter.

MERRY GIFT BOX

Instead of wrapping your Christmas gifts in traditional paper, consider buying white gift boxes and decorating them in holiday colors.

Time: 10 minutes

Materials:
- White gift box
- Red and green markers
- Red and green ribbon

What to Do:

1. Write greetings like "Merry Christmas!" "Season's greetings!" and "Ho, ho, ho!" with a red marker on each side of a white box. Repeat with a green marker.

2. **Tie the box with green ribbon. Finish with a bow.**

3. **Now tie the box with red ribbon. Again, finish with a bow.**

GIFT-BOX COLLAGE

Here's another creative alternative to ordinary gift wrap.

Time: 20 minutes

Materials:
- Old magazines
- Scissors
- Glue
- Gift box

What to Do:

1. Cut an assortment of wintry or holiday-themed pictures from magazines.

2. **Glue the pictures all over a gift box. Overlap them collage-style.**

LOLLIPOP BOUQUET

This is one bouquet everyone will enjoy! It's not only fun to look at, but also fun to eat.

Time: 5 minutes or less

Materials:
- Gift wrap
- Ribbon
- Handful of lollipops (6 or so)
- Scissors

What to Do:

 1. Wrap a gift with gift wrap.

 2. Tie a ribbon around the package. Secure it with a knot.

 3. With the same color ribbon or a coordinating color, tie a handful of lollipops together and knot it tightly, leaving 1 end of the ribbon about 6 inches long.

 4. Tie the bunch of lollipops close to the knot on the package and cut off any excess ribbon.

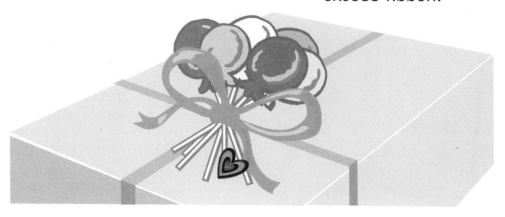

PHOTO GIFT TAG

Instead of writing names on your Christmas gift tags, use photos! You can make use of family pictures that didn't come out right. (Perhaps one person was squinting.) Cut out the nonsquinters and use these photos on the gift tags.

Time: 10 to 15 minutes

Materials:
- 1 photo of the recipient's face
- 1 photo of the giver's face
- Scissors
- Glue
- Pretty paper
- Pen

What to Do:

 1. Find a photo of the recipient and a photo of the giver.

 2. Cut out the faces from the photos.

3. At the top of a small piece of pretty paper, write "to." Glue the recipient's photo next to the word. Just below write "from." Glue the giver's photo next to this word.

TRINKETS ATOP

The recipient of this Christmas gift gets several gifts in one!

Time: 5 minutes

Materials:
- Gift wrap
- Thin ribbon
- Small, lightweight trinkets, such as a plastic whistle, a hair barrette, and so on

What to Do:

 1. Wrap a gift with wrapping paper. Tie the wrapped gift with a thin ribbon. Finish with a bow.

 2. Thread 1 more piece of ribbon under the bow for each trinket you will add.

 3. Tie 1 end of each ribbon to the bow, leaving about 6 inches of ribbon dangling.

 4. Choose a trinket for each ribbon.

 5. Tie the trinkets in place.

3-D SANTA DECORATION

Instead of decorating
Christmas gifts with stickers,
why not make your own package decorations? This Santa
will give any gift box some
holiday spirit!

Time: 15 minutes

Materials:
- Pink and red construction paper
- Scissors
- Pencil
- Glue
- Blue and red markers
- Cotton balls

What to Do:

 1. Cut a circle out of pink paper. This will be Santa's head. The size will depend on the package you're decorating.

2. Draw a stocking cap on red paper. Make it the right size for Santa's head.

3. Cut out the stocking cap.

4. Glue the cap onto Santa's head.

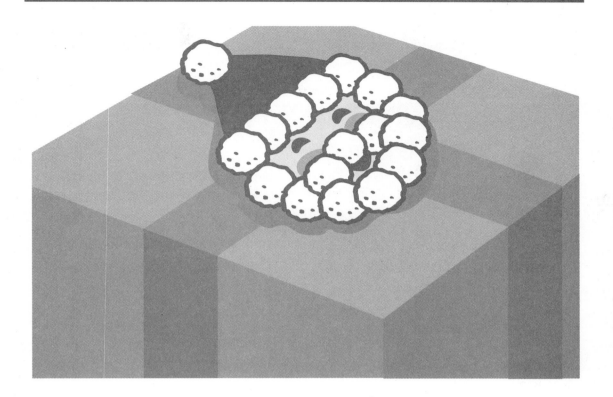

5. Draw Santa's eyes with a blue marker. Use a red marker to make lips and rosy cheeks.

6. Glue a band of cotton balls to the base of the cap. Glue more cotton to the tip for a pompom. Give Santa a cotton beard and mustache, too.

7. Glue your Santa onto a package.

KIDS' HOLIDAY FUN

by Penny Warner
Illustrated by Kathy Rogers

Penny Warner's book gives you fun ideas for entertaining your children at 34 different holidays, including New Year's Eve, Valentine's Day, St. Patrick's Day, the Fourth of July, Halloween, and Christmas. Every single month of the year, your family can turn to this comprehensive guide for delicious holiday recipes, decoration suggestions, instructions for fun holiday activities and games, party ideas, and crafts.

Order #6000 $12.00

THE BEST CHRISTMAS PARTY GAMES AND ACTIVITIES

by Bruce Lansky

This holiday game book contains 8 creative, entertaining, holiday-appropriate kids' games and activities. Complete with tear-out duplicate game sheets for 8 siblings and playmates, this book will keep the kids constructively occupied and away from the television.

Order #6066 $3.95

KIDS' PARTY GAMES AND ACTIVITIES

by Penny Warner
Illustrated by Kathy Rogers

This is the most complete guide to party games and activities for kids ages 2–12! It contains illustrated descriptions, instructions, rules, and troubleshooting tips for 300 games and activities (more than triple the number in other books), including traditional and contemporary games, simple and elaborate activities, and ideas for outings, events, and entertainers.

Order #6095 $12.00

KIDS' OUTDOOR PARTIES

by Penny Warner
Illustrated by Laurel Aiello

This book offers 35 outdoor party themes complete with invitations, costumes, decorations, games, activities, food, cake, favors, variations, and helpful hints. The parties can be thrown in your backyard, a park, or any other outdoor space.

Order #6045 $8.00

THE KIDS' PICK-A-PARTY BOOK

by Penny Warner
Illustrated by Laurel Aiello

Here are 50 creative theme parties to make birthdays and other celebrations so much fun, kids won't want to leave the party. Warner provides themed ideas for invitations, decorations, costumes, games, activities, food, and party favors to help parents make celebrations memorable and entertaining.

Order #6090 $9.00

Order Form

Qty.	Title	Author	Order No.	Unit Cost (U.S. $)	Total
	Bad Case of the Giggles	Lansky, B.	2411	$16.00	
	Best Birthday Party Game Book	Lansky, B.	6064	$3.95	
	Best Christmas Party Games & Activities	Lansky, B.	6066	$3.95	
	Best Halloween Party Games & Activities	Lansky, B.	6067	$3.95	
	Free Stuff for Kids	Free Stuff Editors	2190	$5.00	
	Just for Fun Party Games and Activities	Warner, P.	6065	$3.95	
	Kids Are Cookin'	Brown, K.	2440	$8.00	
	Kids' Holiday Fun	Warner, P.	6000	$12.00	
	Kids' Outdoor Parties	Warner, P.	6045	$8.00	
	Kids' Party Cookbook	Warner, P.	2435	$12.00	
	Kids' Party Games and Activities	Warner, P.	6095	$12.00	
	Kids' Pick-a-Party Book	Warner, P.	6090	$9.00	
	Kids Pick the Funniest Poems	Lansky, B.	2410	$16.00	
	Miles of Smiles	Lansky, B.	2412	$16.00	
	Mommy's Little Helper Christmas Crafts	MacGregor, C.	2445	$8.00	
	New Adventures of Mother Goose	Lansky, B.	2420	$9.95	
	No More Homework! No More Tests!	Lansky, B.	2414	$8.00	
	Poetry Party	Lansky, B.	2430	$12.00	
	Preschooler's Busy Book	Kuffner, T.	6055	$9.95	
	Sweet Dreams	Lansky, B.	2210	$15.00	
				Subtotal	
			Shipping and Handling (see below)		
			MN residents add 6.5% sales tax		
				Total	

YES! Please send me the books indicated above. Add $2.00 shipping and handling for the first book with a retail price up to $9.99 or $3.00 for the first book with a retail price of over $9.99. Add $1.00 shipping and handling for each additional book. All orders must be prepaid. Most orders are shipped within two days by U.S. Mail (7–9 delivery days). Rush shipping is available for an extra charge. Overseas postage will be billed. **Quantity discounts available upon request.**

Send book(s) to:

Name _____ Address _____

City _____ State _____ Zip _____

Telephone (_____)_____

Payment via:

❑ Check or money order payable to Meadowbrook Press (No cash or CODs please)

❑ Visa (for orders over $10.00 only)   ❑ MasterCard (for orders over $10.00 only)

Account # _____ Signature _____ Exp. Date _____

A *FREE* Meadowbrook Press catalog is available upon request.
You can also phone or fax us with a credit card order.

Mail to: Meadowbrook Press
5451 Smetana Drive, Minnetonka, MN 55343
Toll-Free: 800-338-2232

Phone: 612-930-1100

Fax: 612-930-1940

For more information (and fun) visit our website:
www.meadowbrookpress.com